W9-DGY-288

Are You My Dog?

by Marybeth Mataya
Illustrated by Matthew Williams

Content Consultant:
Gerald Brecke
Doctor of Veterinary Medicine

magic
wagon

Are You My
Pet?

visit us at www.abdopublishing.com

Text by Marybeth Mataya
Illustrations by Matthew Williams
Edited by Jill Sherman
Interior layout and design by Emily Love
Cover design by Emily Love

Library of Congress Cataloging-in-Publication Data
Mataya, Marybeth.
Are you my dog? / by Marybeth Mataya ; illustrated by Matthew Williams ; content consultant, Gerald Brecke.
     p. cm. — (Are you my pet?)
  Includes index.
  ISBN 978-1-60270-243-1
  1. Dogs—Juvenile literature. I. Williams, Matthew, 1971- ill. II. Title.
  SF426.5.M276 2009
  636.7—dc22

                          2008003650

Note to Parents/Guardians:
This book can help you teach your child how to be a kind, responsible dog owner. Even so, a child will not be able to handle all the responsibilities of having a pet, so we are glad that you will oversee the responsibility. Neutering or spaying your dog is a key step in helping reduce pet overpopulation and the many homeless and abused pets.

Table of Contents

Is a Dog the Right Pet for Me?

Do you like soggy dog kisses? Do you like a wagging tail? Do you like to go running and walking?

A dog needs a lot of care. Are you someone who can give a lot of care? A dog may be just the pet for you!

Pet Fact:

A dog likes to be part of a pack. Your dog's pack includes you!

Should My Dog Be Big or Small?

Your dog will need a place to run and play. Some people use a fenced yard. Some people take their dogs to parks to play. A big dog needs a lot of room. A small dog needs less room.

Some people are allergic to dogs. When choosing your dog, have all family members spend time with it. You do not want to find out that someone is allergic after you have brought your dog home.

Pet Fact:

If a puppy has big paws, watch out! It may grow into a big dog.

What Kind of Dog Would Be Best?

There are many kinds, or breeds, of dogs. Some like to hunt, such as terriers. Some like to run, such as greyhounds. Some dogs are mixes, or "mutts." They can have the traits of many breeds.

Your parents can help you pick your dog. So can books and Web sites. Animal shelters take care of animals without homes. People there can help you pick a dog, too.

Pet Fact:

There are more than 400 breeds of dogs. Long-haired breeds shed more hair than short-haired breeds.

How Old Should My Dog Be?

Puppies are cute. But, puppies like to chew on things. They do not know how to behave. They do not even know where to poop! It takes a lot of time to train a puppy.

Older dogs do not chew as much. They often know where to poop. Puppies may seem more fun at first, but they are more work.

Pet Fact:

Visit a veterinarian as soon as you get your dog.

What Does My Dog Need?

Your dog will need a dish for food and another for water.

Your dog also will need a soft, safe bed. You can put the bed outside or inside. An outside bed needs shade from the sun. It needs shelter from the rain and cold.

Your dog needs to play and go for walks. Always walk your dog with an adult.

Pet Fact:

Dogs love toys! Some toys can hurt your dog. Ask your veterinarian for a list of safe toys.

What Should I Feed My Dog?

Your dog probably wants to eat everything! But not all food is good for your dog. Do not feed your dog from the table. Your dog needs dog food. The package can tell you how much to feed your dog.

Puppies eat four meals a day. A grown dog should have only one meal, or two small meals. Too much food can make your dog chubby and sad.

Pet Fact:

Dogs need fresh, clean water all day, every day.

How Do I Get to Know My Dog?

At first, your dog is a bundle of barks, yelps, wags, and jumps. Learn your dog's signs. Watch your dog's face and tail.

If your dog's ears are up, your dog is listening and watching you. If your dog's tail is wagging, your dog is happy.

A dog may bite if it is upset. If your dog snarls or growls, back away. If your dog's ears are back, back away. These signs mean your dog is angry or scared. Let your dog rest.

Pet Fact:

Loud noises may scare your dog. Make sure your dog has a safe place it can go when it is scared.

How Do I Teach My Dog?

Your dog needs to be trained. You are the leader of your dog's pack. Your dog wants to make you happy. Praise your dog for sitting or lying down. Offer your dog a treat.

For bad things, frown. Say "no" in a strong voice. Make a sign with your hand, such as a thumbs-down. Do not look at your dog. Your dog will feel sad and want to do better.

These tips are just a start to training your dog. You can take a training class with your dog for more advice.

Pet Fact:

Do not hit your dog. The dog will be hurt and confused. Hitting does not teach.

How Do I Keep My Dog Safe?

Put a collar on your dog. The tag needs your dog's name and your name, address, and phone number. Keep your dog in your yard or on a strong leash.

Watch what your dog eats. Keep chocolate, bones, milk, garlic, onions, raisins, grapes, salt, and candy away from your dog! Some plants can make your dog sick, too.

Ask an adult to put cleaning bottles away. Keep trash can lids shut tight. If your dog looks sick, visit the veterinarian. Bring your dog to the veterinarian for a checkup each year.

Pet Fact:

Dog walkers must pick up pet poop. Poop can make other dogs sick and no one wants to step in it!

How Do I Stay Safe?

Never touch or pet a dog you do not know. Never go near a dog's food when it is eating. A dog needs space. Do not put your face near its face.

With love and care, a dog can live ten to fifteen years. Enjoy this wonderful new friend for life.

Pet Fact:

Dogs need grooming. Brush your dog's fur every day. Ask an adult to clean your dog's teeth, trim its toenails, or give it a bath. They will also need to protect your dog from fleas and ticks.

Words to Know

animal shelter—a safe place for homeless animals.

breed—a specific kind of animal within a species.

groom—to clean oneself to stay healthy.

pack—a family group of animals.

shed—to lose extra hair.

train—to teach an animal rules or tricks.

veterinarian—an animal doctor.

Further Reading

Dennis-Bryan, Kim. *Puppy Care: How to Look After Your Pet*. New York: DK Publishing, 2004.

Evans, Mark. *Puppy: ASPCA Pet Care Guide*. New York: DK Children, 2001.

Landau, Elaine. *Your Pet Dog*. New York: Scholastic, 2007.

Salzmann, Mary Elizabeth. *Dandy Dogs*. Perfect Pets series. Edina: ABDO Publishing Company, 2007.

On the Web

To learn more about dogs, visit ABDO Publishing Company on the World Wide Web at **www.abdopublishing.com**. Web sites about dogs are featured on our Book Links page. These links are routinely monitored and updated to provide the most current information available.

Index